And God Created Women

AND GOD CREATED WOMEN

poems

CONNIE VOISINE

DURHAM, NORTH CAROLINA

And God Created Women
Copyright ©2018 by Connie Voisine.

Library of Congress Cataloging-in-Publication Data
Voisine, Connie.
And God Created Women / by Connie Voisine
p. cm.

ISBN-13: 978-1-4951-7881-8

Published in the United States of America

Cover design: Spock and Associates
Artwork: Svala Olafsdottir
Interior design: Hannah West with Spock and Associates

Published by
BULL CITY PRESS
1217 Odyssey Drive
Durham, NC 27713
www.BullCityPress.com

Table of Contents

Acknowledgements

Shadowgraph Quarterly: "Via Dolorosa" (as "Arcadia")

North Dakota Quarterly: "Starring Brigitte Bardot" and "(Her) Middle Ages" (as "The Middle Ages")

The New Yorker: "Messenger Star"

Zocalo Public Square: "The Devotions" (as "Hate's Body")

The Rumpus: "No, Dog", "Shameful," and "Self-Portrait as Sphinx"

The New Ohio Review: "And God Created Woman"

Many thanks to the journals and magazines in which these poems first appeared. Thanks also to the February Poets Club, started by Jane Medved and Marcela Sulak, for whom many of these were written.

Via Dolorosa

What I took to be a sweet little toad
with the kindest of smiles
turned out to be my awkward yearbook photo
when I had not yet done anything wrong, really.

What I took to be my yearbook photo
turned out to be a ticket to a movie about a girl
who indirectly causes a car crash, a dying.

What I took to be a ticket
turned out to be some kind of evil sprite
who might fill my mouth with cement,

and what I thought was merely a gap
in my memory turned out to be an impossible
chasm into which my meager beauties disappeared.

The baby I saw crawling across
the four-lane highway turned out to be a coyote
with a crooked leg, while the loss of a friend
turned out to be only the first chapter.

Shameful

to have fucked up
your day by my body in
those old pink sweatpants
that don't fit and are stained
from a cooking accident
on the thighs. It's my fault
I have not kept up the dye
job and my roots are dull,
gray and inching towards
the ends. This belly fat
is about 6 years old
now, and the spots are from
an aging situation I inherited
from all my pale ancestors
who only recently emerged
from the forests we were banished to
by history, poverty, an act of murder
(long ago) and other bad luck,
real and imagined. I know
I could try to be someone else,
like a person on TV, perhaps,
but the only shows I watch
are English these days and
about the unfortunate,
where actors have yellowish
teeth and red eyes. *No wonder*,
you'd say, and I am only ashamed
in some distant, uninvolved way.

It's not personal, I'd say
about my body if
you and I were actually able to speak, *it's*
more like a kind of darkness
or artichoke. I can imagine
your laugh if I'd said that.
It's craziness, really, that part
I secretly feel I must kill to survive,
to call that after a vegetable
which is actually a variety of thistle
(the roots are called suckers!).
If I could hold hands with you
on public transport,
beside the woman who smelled
different from any of my people,
the man who said mother-
fucker many times in various
places in one long sentence
into a phone beside a strollered
and beribboned baby (pierced ears)
who twitched in her guileless
sleep, and then if you could say
I am hateful and despairing,
I'd console: *we all are too.*

The Devotions

Hate gives all its reasons
as if they were terms for something more
I would do to you with a foot or a shovel.
There is a certain peace in hate, a clear mountain
that's high with a whitewashed H
on its side which is all mine.
The road is circular and steep,
the stones roll onto it and the plants are
low and ground-hugging and often
appear to be dead. When I walk it
I am always surprised
at how the road drops off at the edge
and how the garbage of others, not mine,
stuns the land. The views are
enormous and belittle.
I would take you there,
I have already many times
thought about it but you are lazy
and ungenerous of yourself and your time.
The last stretch is the most tiring.
I have seen some people sprint all of a sudden,
laughing like it's a game. Not me.
It's a long, ugly slog and the wind hits hard from
all sides once I clear the last corner.
At the top there are two things:
a telescope with a locked door
for all the scientists of hate, not me,
and an altar for the pilgrims,
which is wrecked and ugly, the silk flowers faded
and the votives filled with dust or water.

I saw a tarantula there, so lovely and slow
with her haired segments.
I saw a snake once, too, its rattle woke
the bottom of my brain.
How I hated what she taught me.

Self-Portrait as Medic

I am stained by this war,
and who wouldn't be,
staggering into the traffic
in the square, blood soaking
my uniform, my mind poured out.

How to say what I could have
asked for instead— a vase? A lovely scarf?
How can I return to being
pale, freckled and wanting?

You are my duty and my dulling;
it's a row of you moaning.
I hold all your greasy heads.
I change my clothes, a little

more gone in the hourglass,
in my shoes, in the radio,
in the surgery, blood soaking
the beloved warm and I love

your wounds more than my own,
soldiers, with my clean hands,
fresh apron, my neatly
skewered curls and cap. All I have
is yours. I bathe you again

in my drum of ribs, my cup
of skull. I recall how the saint
buried alive is released
to be buried again in the
hagiography, or, rather,

manual for losing beautifully.

Messenger Star

The tree was dead in my neighbor's yard,
    the branches empty of leaves and the owl's nest
naked and derelict, it seems. We sat with

    our winter picnic and watched for the pair
who haunted our block. The male much smaller
    and loud, staking his dominion just after dark.

The female silent, close by. They seemed like
    glamorous friends, distant but always there.
I'd seen one only once during the daytime.

    I stood at the curb talking to the handyman, when
the female owl came low out the alleyway flying
    soundless, so close I could see her eye

in her pale face, the beak curved and clear,
    but her eye, a killer's, make no mistake, told me
if by any chance of size or opportunity, she would.

    I will not think this was some kind of portent,
that she was a harbinger of all that followed.
    The handyman, always I paid him more

and more, too shy was he to ask his worth, whispered,
    what's wrong, bird? My vegetables would bolt
that spring, a dear friend showed how empty

she saw my love, and another died. He drank
beyond what his body wanted and then he drank
         again. Higginson said of Poe's face, it had *the look*

*of oversensitiveness which when uncontrolled may
         prove more debasing than coarseness.*
I see how this owl could be seen as a sign.

         I was shaking afterward. That bird was roused
terribly from sleep, no doubt, as big as a stump
         and flying. A bat at daytime has a different eye,

naked, but frightened, I once found five under
         a wall clock on the porch and they were blinking
and slow to scatter. Their guano had choked

         the battery. Poe recited poems drunk, revenge?
—he'd say that he had written them when he was ten
         and maybe this was fear, because some of us

only grow more vulnerable to drink, to age; there is less
         ease as we near the end. *A singular music*
wrote Higginson of Poe's voice when he recited

         "The Raven." *What's wrong, bird?*
We spread out blankets on the dry grass and our laps,
         and ate our food, pulled from a faded train case

I found years ago at a curb. It had a diamond-
        shaped mirror. The game and the feeling
was that we were on a journey. The child saw her first,

        at the top of the neighbor's dead tree,
one that would fall on our roof and end in legal action.
        We could not see her mate; she was alone,

so sharply drawn by streetlight we could see her horns.

Self-Portrait as Sphinx

Full means dispose of yourself,
that there are things like mountains,
disease, and geometry, older and bigger
than you but not me, asshole.

Listen is when the wind starts
the ominous purring in the trees,
the butter in the pan, and what I thought
the safety of these rocks above it all.

Hole is my riddle and anxious
and why, the page read and re-, the web
that laces tree, clothesline, the jaws
of the dead, the ones yet to be consumed

by me. *Parting* is what I recognize
with pious humility. Or not. *Shame* is things
look dark tonight and a concluding speech
is what I would have given to my family.

Grove is all hearts and hands and where
I cannot live. I knew not where to find myself there.
Strewn is when he will take the brooches
from his dead wife's breast.

Strewn is a finger in the soil, the seed
pressed through, too deep, anxious and why.
Shame is a rotten tooth. *Strewn* is me,
not human, not any one thing, who must

accept the awful answer. And who
were you—some immigrant, some punk
with gorgeous hair and a temper. *Blind*
also is knowledge that decimates.

And God Created Woman

He made her some great hair,
full of body and a lovely reddish-blonde,
and then he gave her great tits—
large and ebullient,
like twins of a gazelle that feed
among the lilies, actually.
He made her smell fresh as lilies
and a few other things like
Summer Mist, Sweet Romance.
Her bed was green, it was said.
And then he gave that #1 3-D
printer, her womb, but he gave
her only one, unfortunately,
with which to produce the loads
of progeny to be faithful,
inspiring even, to bring wealth
to their families and God. Some
women did not get the hair,
or the chest or a womb programed
to function properly, which became
a management issue. But God created
her eyes to be like those of doves
and she was comforted with apples
and perhaps Cheetos. In the secret places
of the stairs, she eats those Cheetos.

Woman printed out two sons,
in pain she bore them, and later,
much later, that fratricide, another
management fail. God gave her
other wonders, like the flaming

swords barring her from the garden,
a nice set of earrings, and the recent
regional victory of a basketball team.
Much later, God's son was very kind
to her, though she had slipped a bit,
what with the poverty and prostitution.

Neighborhood

The knock—shave
and a haircut—led her
to open the door,
the front door that was
made of wood,
no window, thinking it
was the neighbor,
a jokester, an intimate.
It happened
months ago
and maybe the man before
her meant no harm,
maybe his freckled,
young face and lanky
form was sincere
—she'd had people
from Gospel Rescue
Mission knock, wanting
work, or food, a blanket
once, these ghosts
of need that floated
through her daily life, ones
made of air, until
the hand shook, or stink
of his jeans wafted,
or the story
emerged about a bus ticket
to Amarillo, the baby
and its fucking mother,
and maybe he will go
to Amarillo,

and maybe not.
Terrible the moments of
belief, trust, when you open
your face
to a stranger. Because
you are tired
of your mean self. Because
you remember your own
poverty. Because you
thought it was
someone else. She was settling
her child down
with food, a winter
afternoon in the desert, precise
sun, a leaf blower
somewhere moaning.
The child was eating
slowly, her eyes
in a book about fairies choosing
a mortal life for
reasons of love and loyalty.
Other kids
from the Boys & Girls Club
chattering down the sidewalk
towards the park
disappeared in the
blower's drone
which sounded
like a man's grief,
an unmitigated sadness
from his gut to his throat

and over the public
spaces of the rundown
neighborhood where dogs
chewed at chain link
and once her husband, at
dawn, walking the girl
in his arms when she
was a baby with
colic, found a man
in the gazebo
with a shotgun. She had been
standing on the porch,
watching them, drying
her own tears in a milk-stained
nightgown, who would
see her? and did she care?
The man had said I am
in a bad bad way.
She saw them talking,
the baby had stopped crying
as if she felt the
moment. The man had said
I am going to do something
I will be sorry for
and my license and papers
are in that car. I've got
my baby here,
said her husband and as
he backed away,
he said, I know
there are reasons

for not doing this.
Once in the house,
the small family
lay on the floor
as the man shot himself and
the sirens found
the bright red stain, the body
fallen on the path.
The wedding booked for
that afternoon
went on as planned,
a neighbor's bride
in white, the retinue
of girls in blossom shades
scattering petals
ahead of her. I realized,
a friend of hers once told her,
that I was
planning to cut
my own hand off—the when,
the how, and how not to
die from it, but just to do it
and get it over with. That's when
I called my neighbor.
Her friend survived
and she wishes
she could say that he's not still
suffering or that this man
at the door was in pain
for this reason or that—one he could
retch, spit out. The thing

about the man
at the door was he
seemed in shock, his voice strangely
loud when he spoke and
he wanted to know if Sergio
was home. As if Sergio
could contain his body
which was young
and thin and sewed with ink, shapes
askew up his neck.
Or to put it another way,
the death in a person
was drawn
on his skin, for another's
eyes, the hope being
the death inside might
be assuaged by a face that looks
clearly and directly,
that says what?
how? may I? She looked
at him and thought
of her beautiful
boy in high school who loved
to get high, how he's
been dead now a year,
found in his bed
in Aspen where he
made snow for a living.
How still was the snow day
a week ago—
the cacti covered

in it, the day and night
of waiting
for the melt since there were
no plows, the
dirty, stunted snowmen
that populated the park
were pocked with sticks
and debris, awkward
expressions of joy, opportunity, delirium.
Not very sturdy,
nor long-lived. No one drove,
no one wandered
the streets looking for
what they needed that day,
no one risked crashing,
confrontation or shame.
The street was white
and still. And early
it was very clean, that sacred
blankness associated
with nothingness or the sublime.
It was like the state
her friend's daughter desired for herself
as she ate only blueberries
and peas, as she carved
from her body a self
that was not body, not family,
not food or defecation.
No one saw her
orchestrating her patient
pilgrimage towards

oblivion. The horizon of that
is the question—
at fourteen, she wanted a world
that is utterly pure,
a grassy field the right
green, a lushness
made impossible by anything
living or moving,
by weather and drought,
by trees that shed their
dead leaves and branches,
and animals who must
do their business of shitting
and digging and burning
sometimes.

(Her) Middle Ages

I know men who would

       rape you. That's why.

As long as the sea is wild

       and I would burn a boat to hide.

You wouldn't want to see me naked, scarcely if.

I would have wanted to have the next of kin.

       Once.

The easiest thing to make a woman

       such as me. Cry. A dead child on the news

       works, which.

Makes me piss my panties and

       I smell different.

I didn't know   we were religious.

Troubles press on every side but I am not   crushed,

       destroyed.

The skin on my hands, under my chin,

over the skin on my stomach, plus scar.

Should try to cook on the days I work, meat

or something. You fat bitch.

Baby pictures make me.

It's a gift. Is I must learn to eat, shut up

and not tell a person   what I think.
Anymore.

Because I won't be forgiven. Why has this happened

to us? Does this

mean a person might die without?

The sea collects in small pools of. A daughter is hard

on her mother.

Never done fear. Although not young.

Since you started all this shit.

I had hair down

to the pockets of my jeans.

It's too hot in here, these.

Chicken skin,   chocolate, stinking cheeses,   wine.

My mother never. How credible. Did anyone see

Or notice her when.

Begin the repossession. Drinks too.

No, Dog

The horse is a dreamscape
until I am riding the horse and then it's
muscle and control and a being who really

doesn't want to be me. There are dogs
who want to become a person. KoKo watches
me talk or eat or enter the room with a stare:

"tell me," or "give me," or "touch me," much
the way my daughter could not stop being
with me for years, at the breast, in my arms

on my stomach and inside my bowels. Her
small hands on my face or in my shirt, fingers
in my hair and in my mouth. I did not ask

her to want me so much, I did not know
she would cry at night if she couldn't feel
my skin or even if I left the room early

in the morning to sit alone. The child knows
I am the ladder of her, her face the skull
of all skulls and her teeth the first teeth to

split skin and rip open a plum so fiercely
we laugh as if it's funny. The child hates
the grass, why would she like its scratch and

bump, why would that dry scramble of weed
belong to her foot, her flank, her tiny palms
the texture and size of an opossum's, blindish

and twitching. Her first word is No. Her second
is Mine. She shoves the world into herself
the way the horse's jaws maul and grind

the green. She pulls it out of me and dumps it
behind and she gallops out and through
some churning, unknown river to the other side.

The child is a dreamscape until she wakes that first time, yelling.

Self-Portrait as Cop

I speak on the phone to the criminal,
and I know enough to piss him off. Of course,
I have a secret life too, which he tries
to use against me. These are beautiful streets,

trees lacing what small sky I can see when
I head out to the squad car and my driver.
Sidewalks are always fresh and clean
from the rain, which happens every day

and my heels, impossibly high, do not impede
my progress towards the crime scene.
Regaining consciousness in the hospital,
the victim says that anyone looking in

the window would see me tied up and
I tell her that anyone who has spoken
has felt better for doing it. Which means
I lie when it suits me. Why tell anyone

your mysteries? Why play a piano that
needs tuning, play only one note (painful)
as I drink my whiskey? Why can no one else
remember the right details to catch him

who secretly watched while
they went to the toilet, drank with girl-
friends, hollered about strippers, dropped
a wallet by the greenhouse in the park

where exotics grow? It's hard to work
when your child calls you about the things
that trouble her, dollies forgotten or a dream
involving women with babies in their bodies,

babies who might be, when they are born,
too small to survive. Once the horses in Europe
were large and slow—they called them "cold-
blooded"—and the horses from Asia were fast

little creatures, "hot-blooded." I have tried
to be someone who fixes things, people.
I walk to the crime scene, still quiet,
an old house a young woman bought

and was trying to repair. My underlings
are people I can trust with not much
but punctuality. The country roads cut
corners no one can negotiate at full speed

and there are so many if onlys, says
the victim's sister. The river is so dark, murky,
the divers discover only by touch of their neoprene
gloves. I am cold-blooded, I must be,

slow and large, moving towards him,
that killer, with my long sword and shield,
my children often all night with a sitter,
my unflattering floodlight, my forensics.

Starring Brigette Bardot

Metaphors are hard tonight,
but similes are harder,
they always are. Who can
find an object adequate for
enlightening this empty house?
Or to explain the sadness of
the dull spot of streetlight
on the yellow grass in the park?
Dis-moi quelque chose
de gentil, mon cheri,
is what Bardot sings in
And God Created Woman,
and it's a begging sort of song.
Tell me something nice, my dear.
Brigitte wears only a bikini bottom
on the album cover, she hides
her breasts with her arms.
She's on a recent clickbait list
 "Celebrities Who've Let Themselves Go."
These days, she saves the mutts of Bucharest,
brings them to her country home
for sunshine and food and whatever
love they can bear. I sing,
Prends-moi dans tes bras,
embrace moi, et sourire.
My gate makes a noise
when opened or closed, it clinks now.
A friend might be about to knock
on the door but sometimes
it's a stranger closing what's left open
and walking away. *Clink.*

Tonight I might have to try synecdoche,
The White House says, or *Nice threads,*
Take my heart, where a small part
stands for the whole.

Moon, Tonight

And who has seen the moon, has missed
her awkward approach to the reds and yellows
of the Sun-News Building lights? She's got nothing
on the sunburst crossed with letters crossed
with cold-cathode gas-discharge at the end
of our street. No one says hello tonight, her meek
halo dispersed among the halogen street lamps.
She, pale and numinous, wants nothing
for herself, there are bigger and
more forward items about this night and all

the others. She has no ambition, our moon,
doesn't understand her relationship to any
striving. It's hard enough to lift herself
off the horizon, haul her fattening body
from there to there to there, all the places
she's supposed to be at certain times and
the tides, why that's enough to do right there,
rough and tugging at her chest, needing
to buoy this and feed that and eat the dunes
and beach the whales. She hates doing it.

About the Author

Connie Voisine is the author of the book of poems *Calle Florista*, from University of Chicago Press. Her previous books are *Cathedral of the North*, winner of the AWP Prize for Poetry, *Rare High Meadow of Which I Might Dream*, a finalist for the *Los Angeles Times* Book Award. Her poems have appeared in *The New Yorker, Ploughshares, Poetry Magazine, Black Warrior Review, The Threepenny Review,* and elsewhere. Her book, *The Bower*, is forthcoming in 2019. She lives in New Mexico with her husband and daughter.

http://www.connievoisine.com

This book was published with assistance from the Spring 2018 Editing and Publishing class at the University of North Carolina at Chapel Hill. Contributing editors and designers were Hayes Cooper, Nguyen Le, Deborah Olaniyan, and Hannah West.